some like it **Hot**

50 Drinks to Warm Your Spirits

some like it Hot

· · · *by* Holly Burrows and Katie Walter · · ·

PHOTOGRAPHS BY MAREN CARUSO

CHRONICLE BOOKS
SAN FRANCISCO

TEXT COPYRIGHT © 2005 by *Holly Burrows* and *Katie Walter.*
PHOTOGRAPHS COPYRIGHT © 2005 by *Maren Caruso.*

Library of Congress Cataloging-in-Publication Data available.

ISBN 0-8118-4404-8

Manufactured in China.

Designed by *Jay Peter Salvas*
Food and prop styling by *Kim Konecny* and *Erin Quon*
Photo assistant: *Faiza Ali*
This book was typeset in Matrix 11/12, Matrix Script, and Meta Plus 8/11

Distributed in Canada by Raincoast Books
9050 Shaughnessy Street
Vancouver, British Columbia, V6P 6E5

10 9 8 7 6 5 4 3 2 1

Chronicle Books LLC
85 Second Street
San Francisco, California 94105

www.chroniclebooks.com

DEDICATION

To our Mothers, who made us our very first hot cocoas, topped with marshmallows and filled with love.

ACKNOWLEDGMENTS

Thanks to David and John, our full-time tasters and tech guys. To Sarah, Judy, and Lorraine, our dedicated helpers, who read our many drafts and tested our recipes, good and bad. And thanks to little Libby for all her help with banging pots and pans during our many taste-testing sessions.

We never could have done this without everyone at Chronicle Books. Thank you to Bill LeBlond and Amy Treadwell for giving us the opportunity to do our first book. We truly appreciate all of your trust, patience, and guidance. Many thanks to Rebecca Pepper for her thoroughness, Jan Hughes and Doug Ogan for their careful edits, Laurel for her encouraging words, Jay Peter Salvas for his creativity and flexible collaboration, and Yolanda Accinelli in production for bringing it all together. Finally, thank you to Maren, Kim, and Erin, for making our drinks more beautiful than we ever imagined.

Contents

INTRODUCTION

Every year it happens. The warm breezes and sweet scents of summer give way to the crisp autumn air and the smell of fallen leaves. The nights grow longer, the temperatures fall, and before we know it, the winter winds are howling and snow and ice are covering the ground. But just because the tiki torches are doused and the only flames burning are those in the fireplace, now is not the time for hibernation. 'Tis the season for celebration!

The fall harvest and the winter holidays provide the perfect backdrop for good times. Whether you're relaxing with close friends or hosting the whole extended family, hot drinks are a great alternative to the same old holiday fare. In the dead of winter, wouldn't you rather warm up with a hot concoction than an icy cocktail or frosty mug of beer? We know we would. The problem has always been figuring out what to serve instead.

While endless books full of cool, fruity, ice-filled summer cocktails line the shelves of our favorite bookstores, we could never find a book of unique and delicious recipes for hot drinks to take us from the harvest through the holidays. So we set out to create our very own collection of recipes for seasonal sips. Some are classics, and some we've concocted. We've included spirited libations as well as a sprinkling of nonalcoholic drinks. From ridiculously simple drinks for cozy nights at home to make-ahead batches to dazzle friends and family, you'll find a hot drink for every occasion.

When the season's activities take you outside, toting along hot drinks will keep you and yours warm and toasty. Make home-coming unique this year—host a Toddy Tailgate with Hottie Toddies, Amaretto Sour Toddies, and Pear Ginger Toddies. Even raking leaves in the backyard or shoveling snow from the front walk is better when followed by a warm Caramel Apple Sip or a rich Hot Cocolat. And after a day of hitting the slopes, warm up with a steaming Kiss Me I'm Irish Coffee, or end a serious session of sledding with a White Hot Mint. Nothing feels better than coming in from the cold, wrapping your frozen fingers around a warm mug, and letting a sweet, steaming potion warm up your numb nose and chapped cheeks.

Once the holidays roll around and you're swamped with shopping lists and holiday open houses, you can still be the holiday hostess with the mostest. Bring the heat inside and host a hot cocktail party with Cinnamon Cider Martinis, Hotsicles, and Baninis. Serve Mulled Apple Cider on Thanksgiving, stir up nostalgia with a big bowl of rich, warm Eggnog on Christmas Day, or break from tradition and celebrate Mexican-style with a batch of Ponche, or in the spirit of the Scandinavians with Glögg. From a simple supper followed by a sensational Café Dolores to a Just Desserts party complete with luscious liquid versions of Tiramisù and Bananas Foster, you will find that hot drinks offer endless ideas for simple yet memorable entertaining.

Even as the holidays wind down, hot drinks are a perfect cure for the winter doldrums. You'll actually look forward to waking up when you know that a steaming mug of Lavender Vanilla Cream awaits you. If you're looking for that late afternoon pick-me-up, a Spiced Chai Tea will do the trick. And on those nights that are perfect for cuddling up with a good book in front of a roaring fire, brew a cup of fragrant Lemon Ginger Tea or Heavenly Hibiscus.

Whatever the occasion, we hope this collection of our favorite hot drink recipes will warm your autumn outings and add sparkle to your holiday gatherings. These treats can become part of your family traditions—the drinks you share as you carve the family pumpkin, huddle to keep warm at the Thanksgiving Day parade, or deck the halls with holiday cheer. So from the first frost to the early signs of spring, from the frantic holiday celebrations to all those times you need some soul-soothing in between, throw on your party shoes or pull on your fuzzy sweater, and heat things up with *Some Like It Hot.*

Equipment

Making hot drinks is easy when you have the right tools on hand. Here are a few essentials.

Coffee Grinder

Ideal for the at-home grind, this handy tool grinds coffee as well as spices, nuts, and dried fruits. Try grinding coffee beans together with your favorite spices to create a unique flavored coffee.

Coffeemaker

For delicious coffee drinks, you'll need a coffeemaker or European coffee press. Whichever brewing method you choose, make sure your coffee is ground accordingly: medium for a coffeemaker, fine for a coffee press.

Ladle

A ladle, especially one with a pouring spout, makes transferring hot drinks from saucepan to servingware a breeze.

Measuring Cups

You'll want a set of dry measuring cups for measuring sugar and other dry ingredients. You'll also want 1-, 2-, and 4-cup tempered glass liquid measuring cups. They're perfect for drinks that are heated in the microwave instead of on the stovetop.

Measuring Spoons

Any standard set should measure up.

Pots and Pans

Small saucepans are ideal for single servings, and large saucepans are best for bigger batches. If you're doubling a recipe, use a stockpot. For easier serving, use saucepans with spouts or lipped rims, which prevent drips when pouring. If you don't have such pans, transferring your hot drink into a glass measuring cup will make it much easier to pour, especially when you're serving your drinks in rimmed or narrow-mouthed glasses such as champagne flutes.

Shot Glasses

Look for ones with $1/2$-, 1-, and $1 1/2$-ounce markings to add a little this or that.

Stirring Tools

Any spoon will do. However, for hot drinks containing chocolate or other stir-intensive additions, a small wire whisk works wonders.

Strainers

These indispensable little gadgets make it easy to strain spices, seeds, and other solids from drinks so all that's left behind is the liquid libation, full of wonderful flavors. A small strainer works well for single servings, while a large one comes in handy for larger batches.

Servingware

What's the fun of whipping up an exotic hot drink without having something to show it off in? Keep the following on hand and you'll always be prepared.

Mugs, Cups, and Glasses

Though hot drinks do just fine in your favorite mug, why not get creative with some of the fancier, more festive drinks? Whichever servingware you choose, make sure it can take the heat! Ensure that any glass you use is tempered and that porcelain, ceramic, and earthenware are heat resistant. And to keep things easy, make sure your servingware is dishwasher and microwave safe.

Ceramic mugs and Irish coffee glasses are ideal for casual drinks like cocoas and teas. Incredibly rich and sweet dessert drinks are best served in espresso or demitasse cups.

Martini glasses, wine glasses, and flutes allow for a more elegant presentation of hot cocktails and after-dinner drinks. Remember that concoctions served in these types of glasses are meant to be served *warm* rather than steaming hot. Additionally, tempering your glass with hot water before adding the warm liquid is always a good idea.

Thermal Containers

To take hot drinks on the road, thermal carafes or air pots are the way to go. Available in various sizes and styles, they keep liquids hot and make serving a breeze. For large gatherings such as tailgates, insulated beverage coolers with built-in serving spouts are ideal.

Tureens and Slow Cookers

Batches of hot drinks look magnificent on your holiday table when displayed in elegant and decorative tureens. With backup batches on the stove for periodically refilling the tureen, guests are guaranteed a steady supply of warm drinks. For more casual gatherings, let guests serve themselves directly from the stovetop or from the nonstop heat of a slow cooker.

INGREDIENTS

Experts always say you shouldn't cook with a wine you wouldn't drink. Well, the same principle applies to hot drinks: quality in, quality out. With the following ingredients on hand, you'll be prepared to create any of your favorite hot drinks.

BASICS

Apples, lemons, limes, and oranges

Baking soda*

Blueberries and raspberries*

Butter

Caramel sauce

Chocolate: bittersweet, milk, semisweet, white

Cocoa powder, unsweetened

Coconut milk

Coffee beans

Eggs

Espresso powder or instant coffee*

Figs*

Flavored syrups: crème de menthe, raspberry*

Fruit juices: apple cider, cranberry, grape, orange, peach nectar, pear nectar, pomegranate, plum, pineapple, white grape

Graham crackers*

Half-and-half, heavy whipping cream, whole milk, 2 percent milk

Honey

Marshmallows

Molasses*

Raisins*

Sugar: brown, white, superfine

Sweetened condensed milk*

Sweet sherry

Teas: black tea such as Darjeeling or Earl Grey; green tea; herbal tea such as cranberry apple and mint

Tonic water*

SPICES AND HERBS

Allspice berries

Cardamom pods

Chipotle powder*

Cinnamon, sticks and ground

Cloves, whole and ground

Ginger, fresh and ground

Hibiscus flowers, dried*

Lavender flowers, dried*

Mint leaves, fresh

Nutmeg, whole and ground

(continued)

Star anise*

Thyme sprigs*

Vanilla beans

Vanilla extract

BEER, WINE, AND SPIRITS

Amaretto

Amber ale*

Anisette

Applejack brandy*

B & B*

Baileys Irish cream

Bourbon*

Brandy

Chambord

Champagne

Cinnamon schnapps*

Crème de banane

Crème de menthe*

Dark crème de cacao

Frangelico

Gin*

Godiva liqueur

Grand Marnier

Kahlúa

Red wine

Ruby port*

Rum: dark, light, spiced

Tequila*

Vodka

Whiskey

White wine

Used in only one recipe.

Just as the right wrap or a chic handbag can complete an outfit, a colorful garnish can give a hot drink that perfect finishing touch.

Candied Citrus Peel and Ginger

Candied citrus peel and ginger are a delicious accompaniment to juice- or tea-based hot drinks. Skewer them for a fancy and decorative touch, or just float them on the drink to infuse some of the flavor. The instructions are simple. For candied citrus peel, take the peel of a citrus fruit, scraping off as much of the white part (pith) as possible; for ginger, use 1/2 cup peeled, thinly sliced ginger root. Combine 1 cup water and 1 cup sugar in a small sauce-pan and heat over medium-high heat until boiling, stirring until the sugar dissolves. Add the citrus peel or ginger root, reduce the heat to low, and simmer until translucent, 20 to 30 minutes. Remove from the heat and strain, reserving the peel or ginger. Using a fork, shake off any excess water, dredge the peel or ginger in sugar, and gently shake off any excess sugar. Cool completely before using.

Decorative Rims

Rimming a glass with sugar, chocolate, or crushed nuts is yet another way to impart flavor to your drink. Rub the rim of a glass with a wedge of lemon, lime, or orange, or dip it in a shallow dish filled with liqueur, juice, or water. Next, dip the rim in a shallow dish filled with sugar, unsweetened cocoa, shaved cho-colate, or whatever else complements your drink. Gently shake off any excess. It's always fun to experiment. Try using two differ-ent liqueurs or a cinnamon sugar to create more complex flavors.

Dipped Popsicle Sticks

For a fun and kitschy accompaniment to any drink, dress up a Popsicle stick with melted chocolate or caramel. Melt 3/4 cup chopped chocolate or caramel (and 1 tablespoon shortening if you are using chocolate) in a double boiler over medium-high heat. Stir occasionally until melted. Remove from the heat and pour into a shallow dish. Dip in a Popsicle stick, turning to coat two thirds of it. Set on a piece of waxed paper and repeat the process with the remaining Popsicle sticks. Cool in the refrigerator before using.

Flavored Whipped Cream

You probably thought it impossible to improve upon the decadent simplicity of whipped cream. Well, you'd better start believing! With liqueurs, extracts, flavored syrups, or spices to stir in, any flavor is yours for the making. Some of our personal favorites are Kahlúa, lemon juice, ginger (stir in ground ginger), and vanilla extract. Another idea for adding pizzazz is to dust whipped cream with grated spices, grated citrus zest, or cocoa powder or to drizzle it with caramel or chocolate sauce. If you're feeling particularly adventurous, dream up flavor combinations such as mint whipped cream drizzled with chocolate, or Frangelico whipped cream dusted with espresso powder.

Fruit and Citrus Shapes

Using small, decorative cutters, which are essentially small cookie cutters, available at cooking stores, you can press out fun and festive shapes from citrus peels as well as thin slices of apple, pear, or ginger root. Think leaves for autumn, stars for Christmas, or hearts for Valentine's Day. Start with citrus peel or fruit slices thin enough for the cutter to press through. Place the cutter on the peel or slice, press down, and voilà! If you don't have cutters, simple slices can be just as nice. Float the shapes or thread them on decorative skewers or pretty drink umbrellas.

Stenciling

Dress up the kids' cups at their next birthday party, stencil gingerbread men for your Christmas gathering, or show off your team's letters for the big game. Just select a piece of heavy card stock larger than the rim of the mug and, using an X-Acto knife, cut out a stencil in a fun shape or a letter for monogramming. Pour the hot drink into the mug and top with a few small dollops of whipped cream. Allow the whipped cream to melt a bit to create a flat surface. Place the stencil atop the mug and sift cocoa, tinted sugar, or cinnamon over the stencil. Remove the stencil to reveal a unique and personalized drink.

Sugared Berries

Skewer two or three raspberries, cranberries, or other small berries onto a toothpick or decorative skewer. Dip the skewered berries in a small bowl of cold water, gently shake off any excess water, and then dip the skewer into a shallow bowl of sugar to coat. Shake again to remove any excess sugar.

Tinted Sugars

Tinted sugar adds a special touch to your favorite hot drink when used to rim glasses or sprinkled on top of whipped cream. All you need is a small plastic zip-top bag, granulated sugar, and food coloring. Place the desired amount of sugar in the plastic bag, add a few drops of food coloring, and shake to distribute the color evenly. Add more food coloring until you achieve the desired hue.

HOT COCKTAIL HOUR

Whether you're winding down with co-workers or ringing in the holidays with a few close friends, leave behind the noisy crowds of the bars and clubs and bring happy hour home! With these hot twists on your favorite concoctions, hosting a hot, hot, hot cocktail party couldn't be easier.

From martinis to toddies to island-inspired cocktails, these hot drinks will make your happy hour a hit with everyone from beer lovers to mixed drinksters. Serve up steaming glasses of Hot Apple Lager and Hottie Toddies and set out some spiced nuts and chunky pretzels to create a casual atmosphere reminiscent of the neighborhood pub. Or dim the lights, spin some Billie Holiday, and pour Chocolate Martinis for a swankier affair. The best part about hosting a hot cocktail party? Happy hour lasts as long as you want it to!

Serves 1

Hottie Toddy

This bourbon-based and honey-laced toddy
is perfect for cozying up in front of the fire.
On a blustery eve, nothing warms you up better!

FOR EACH DRINK:

2 lemon slices
6 whole cloves
1 1/2 ounces bourbon
1/2 tablespoon freshly squeezed lemon juice
2 teaspoons honey
1/2 cup boiling water
1 cinnamon stick

Stud the lemon slices with the cloves and drop them in the
bottom of an Irish coffee glass. Add the bourbon, lemon juice,
and honey. Slowly stir in the boiling water, using the cinnamon stick and serve.

Serves 4

Cinnamon Cider Martinis

For a sophisticated spin on cider, dress it up for cocktail hour. With a splash of vodka and a cinnamon-sugar rim, this concoction adds a swanky touch to your fall festivities.

CINNAMON-SUGAR RIM

Apple cider

Sugar mixed with a little cinnamon

1 cup apple cider

6 ounces (3/4 cup) Cinnamon-Flavored Vodka
(recipe follows)

Dip the edges of 4 martini glasses in apple cider and rim them with the cinnamon sugar.

In a small saucepan, combine the 1 cup cider and vodka. Heat over medium to medium-high heat until warm but not hot. Pour into the rimmed martini glasses and serve.

CINNAMON-FLAVORED VODKA:

Place 2 cinnamon sticks inside a 1-pint (375 ml) bottle of vodka. You may need to pour out a small amount of the vodka to make room for the cinnamon sticks. Seal tightly and let stand at room temperature for about 2 weeks, depending on the desired level of flavor. Shake the bottle every few days. Remove the cinnamon sticks and use.

Amaretto Sour Toddy

The yin and yang of sweet almond and tart citrus
is why this cocktail has stood the test of time.
Transformed into a toddy and topped with a leaf-shaped piece
of lemon zest, this version has seasonal a-peel.

FOR EACH DRINK:

1/2 **tablespoon freshly squeezed lemon juice**

1/2 **tablespoon freshly squeezed lime juice**

3/4 **teaspoon sugar**

1 **ounce amaretto**

1/2 **cup boiling water**

Leaf shape cut from a strip of lemon zest for garnish (see page 16)

Combine the lemon juice, lime juice, sugar, and amaretto in an Irish coffee glass. Slowly stir in the boiling water, drop in a lemon leaf, and serve.

Chocolate Martinis

Chocolate and the martini — *are there two greater temptations?*
We didn't think so . . . until we tried them together. This sweet
version of the classic cocktail is exquisite.

CHOCOLATE RIM

Godiva liqueur
Shaved milk chocolate or semisweet chocolate

8 ounces (1 cup) Godiva liqueur
4 ounces (1/2 cup) vodka
1/2 cup half-and-half

Dip the edges of 4 martini glasses in liqueur and rim them
with chocolate.

In a small saucepan, combine the liqueur, vodka, and half-and-half.
Heat over medium to medium-high heat until warm but not hot.
Pour into the rimmed martini glasses and serve.

Mojito Mint Tea

For a taste of Old Havana, brew up a little fun
with this hot Cuban cocktail that is **muy** caliente!

FOR EACH DRINK:

2 teaspoons sugar
4 fresh mint leaves
1 teaspoon freshly squeezed lime juice
3/4 cup freshly brewed mint tea

Gently crush the sugar, mint, and lime juice in an Irish coffee
glass, using a muddler or the back of a wooden spoon. Add
the tea and stir. Strain into a fresh Irish coffee glass, discard
the mint, and serve.

Serves 4

Hotsicles

We never outgrow our craving *for that tasty orange and cream
combination—can't you hear the ice cream truck now?
Our warm version of this cool classic,
complete with a Popsicle stick, is a nostalgic addition
to your hot drink repertoire. Little ones will love it, too; just skip
the Grand Marnier.*

2 cups half-and-half

2 cups strained orange juice

4 ounces (1/2 cup) Grand Marnier
(optional)

White chocolate–dipped Popsicle stick for garnish
(see page 15)

Combine the half-and-half, orange juice, and Grand Marnier,
if desired, in a medium saucepan. Heat over medium heat until
warmed. Pour into mugs and serve with white chocolate–
dipped Popsicle sticks.

HOT HINT:

For a frothier texture, whip the mixture with a milk frother or wire whisk
prior to serving.

Cookies 'n' Cream

Santa may never again settle for milk and cookies once he
gets a sip of this sweet delight. Smooth and nutty with a hint of
cinnamon, it has all the flavor of a freshly baked cookie,
sans the crumbs.

8 ounces (1 cup) Baileys Irish cream

8 ounces (1 cup) amaretto

**1/2 teaspoon ground cinnamon, plus additional
for garnish**

Combine the Baileys and amaretto in a small saucepan. Heat
over medium-low heat until warm but not hot. Stir in the
1/2 teaspoon cinnamon. Pour into martini glasses, sprinkle
with cinnamon, and serve.

Pear Ginger Toddies

According to Ralph Waldo Emerson, *there are only ten minutes in the life of a pear when it is perfect to eat. No such rush here. Savor this sweet yet spicy pear concoction anytime.*

2 cups pear nectar

4 whole cloves

$1/2$ teaspoon ground ginger

$1/8$ teaspoon grated nutmeg

1 teaspoon maple syrup

3 ounces ($1/3$ cup) spiced rum

Candied ginger on skewers for garnish
(see page 15)

Combine the pear nectar, cloves, ginger, nutmeg, and syrup in a small saucepan and bring to a simmer over medium-high heat. Reduce the heat to medium and simmer for 5 minutes, stirring occasionally. Remove from the heat, pour into 4 Irish coffee glasses, and add 3/4 ounce rum to each glass. Remove the cloves, garnish with the candied ginger skewers, and serve.

Hot Buttered Rum

Campaigning politicians used this libation *in early America to butter up voters. While traditional recipes call for boiling water, substituting a mulled cider base adds to the sweet and spice of this hottie. So warm your friends and family to the core with a hot buttered rum—you'll certainly get their votes.*

FOR EACH DRINK:

1 twist lemon peel

3 whole cloves

2 ounces dark rum

1 tablespoon brown sugar

2/3 cup apple cider

1 tablespoon butter

1 cinnamon stick

Freshly grated nutmeg for garnish

Stud the lemon peel with the cloves. Combine the studded peel, rum, and brown sugar in a mug. Set aside.

Bring the cider to a boil in a small saucepan over medium-high heat. Remove from the heat and add to the spiced rum mixture. Stir in the butter, using the cinnamon stick. Garnish with a dusting of nutmeg and serve.

Baninis

You say Bellini, I say Banini!
We've put a delicious twist on this popular brunch cocktail by adding
a dash of banana.
Serve it in a champagne flute, adorn with a peach slice, and
you've got one sophisticated concoction.

1 ¹/₃ cups peach nectar
8 ounces (1 cup) champagne, at room temperature
2 ounces crème de banane
4 peach slices for garnish

Heat the peach nectar in a small saucepan over medium-high heat until steaming but not simmering. Pour 2 ounces of champagne and ¹/₂ ounce of crème de banane into each of 4 champagne flutes. Slowly stir ¹/₃ cup peach nectar into each flute, drop in a peach slice, and serve.

HOT HINT:

While we usually recommend heating drinks served in more delicate glassware only until warm, you do want to heat the peach nectar until it's hot for this drink, as you're adding it to champagne and crème de banane, which are at room temperature. Hot nectar will guarantee a warm, yummy Banini.

Serves 4

Hot Apple Lagers

With only two ingredients, *both of which you probably have on
        hand, this is a quick drink to whip up for those unexpected guests.
But don't be surprised if they linger over the lager.*

4 cups apple cider
1 bottle (12 ounces) amber ale, at room temperature

Heat the cider in a medium saucepan over medium-high heat
until reduced by one third, about 15 minutes. Remove from the
heat and slowly add the ale. Pour into large mugs and serve.

HOT HINT:

If your ale is cold when you add it, return the mixture to the stovetop
and warm it over medium heat for about 1 minute before serving. Or for
a variation, replace the amber ale with white wine for a Hot Apple Vino.

. . . Serves 2 or 4

Red Hot Santas

This drink is reminiscent of yummy Red Hots
candies. What a jolly way to warm your insides. You go, Santa!

2 ounces Frangelico
4 ounces (1/2 cup) cinnamon schnapps
1/2 cup half-and-half

GARNISH

Whipped cream
Red cinnamon candies

In a small saucepan, combine the Frangelico, cinnamon schnapps, and half-and-half. Heat over medium to medium-high heat until warm but not hot. Pour into 2 martini glasses or 4 demitasse cups, top with dollops of whipped cream, sprinkle with red cinnamon candies, and serve.

HOT HINT:

Petite drinks like Red Hot Santas can also be served in newly purchased votive candleholders. Votives are more widely available than demitasse cups and come in many festive colors and styles, especially around the holidays. You can't hold a candle to them!

HARVEST HOTTIES & FALL FLINGS

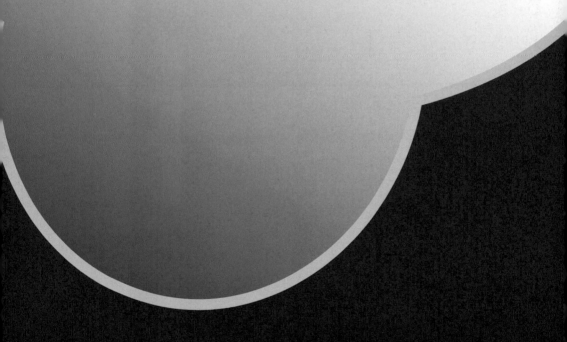

Fall is here! What better time to gather
with friends and family to usher in
autumn over steaming drinks?
From mulled ciders to spiced wines to seasonal
sweets, there's a trick and a treat
for every guest, ghoul, and goblin.

Mulled Apple Cider is sure to be a winner at any homecoming tailgate
(even if your team isn't), while gooey S'more Meltaways are perfect
for your pumpkin-carving party. A long, chilly hayride through the fall
colors of the apple orchard is the perfect occasion for savoring a
Caramel Apple Sip. And let the aromas of Mulled, Mulled Wine and
Orange Cardamom Coffee welcome guests into your home for a
Wednesday-before-Thanksgiving get-together. We can't think of a better
way to celebrate the season's holidays and warm up all those crisp
days and nights in between.

Pumpkin Potion No. 9

*Dinner is over and everyone's ready for dessert. You could let them eat pie,
but why not try something different? This rich, spiced drink
with all the flavors of
pumpkin pie is delicious topped with ginger whipped cream.
No Thanksgiving leftovers here!*

GINGER WHIPPED CREAM

1 cup heavy whipping cream

2 tablespoons sugar

1 teaspoon ground ginger

4 cups 2 percent or whole milk

1/2 cup plus 2 tablespoons sugar

1/2 cup plus 2 tablespoons pumpkin pie filling

1/2 teaspoon pumpkin pie spice

To make the ginger whipped cream: In a medium bowl, beat the
whipping cream, sugar, and ginger until peaks form. It can be
prepared 1 day ahead and stored in the refrigerator; whisk before
serving. Makes 2 cups.

Combine the milk, sugar, pie filling, and pie spice in a medium
saucepan over medium to medium-high heat, stirring to dissolve

the pie filling. Continue heating until steaming but not simmering. Remove from the heat and pour into mugs. Serve topped with dollops of ginger whipped cream. Reserve the remaining whipped cream for another use.

HOT HINT:

You can buy pumpkin pie spice in the spice aisle at the grocery store, or make it yourself by combining equal parts ground cinnamon, nutmeg, allspice, cloves, and ginger.

Serves 4

Hot Cocolat

The terms "hot cocoa" and "hot chocolate" are often used interchangeably, but they are technically two different hot drinks. Hot cocoa is prepared using cocoa powder; hot chocolate is prepared using chocolate bars melted into a cream. In this recipe we've captured the best of both worlds; hence the name Hot Cocolat!

4 cups 2 percent or whole milk
1 cup chopped milk chocolate
2 tablespoons unsweetened cocoa powder

GARNISH

Whipped cream or marshmallows
Unsweetened cocoa powder

Bring the milk to a simmer in a medium saucepan over medium to medium-high heat. Add the chocolate and cocoa powder. Whisk until the chocolate has melted. Simmer for an additional minute, whisking continuously. Remove from the heat and pour into mugs. Top with dollops of whipped cream or marshmallows, sprinkle with cocoa powder, and serve.

HOT HINT:

For a festive touch, sprinkle with tinted sugars (see page 17) instead of cocoa. Try spooky orange for Halloween, merry red and green for Christmas, cool blue for Hanukkah, or romantic red for Valentine's Day.

Mulled Apple Cider

Nothing is more inviting than the aroma of sweet apple cider and mulling spices filling your home. This mixture captures the traditional warmth of cinnamon and cloves but also has an unexpected hint of citrus.

12 cups apple cider

1/4 cup orange juice

2 teaspoons grated lemon zest

2 teaspoons grated orange zest

1/4 cup brown sugar

4 cinnamon sticks

4 whole cloves

2 whole allspice berries

Pinch of freshly grated nutmeg

Pinch of salt

1 1/2 cups applejack brandy (optional)

12 cinnamon sticks for garnish

Mix all the ingredients except the brandy and cinnamon sticks in a large saucepan over medium-high heat. Bring to a boil. Reduce the heat and simmer for 30 minutes. Remove from the heat, strain, and discard the solids. Add the brandy, if desired. Ladle into mugs and serve with cinnamon sticks.

Winter White Sangría

Sangría brings to mind wild and crazy Cinco de Mayo
celebrations and pitchers overflowing with ice and fruit. But just because it's
cold outside doesn't mean your fiesta should take a siesta.
We've created a hot, herbal take on this summer favorite
that's perfect for serving along
with Latino-themed appetizers.

3/4 cup sugar

3 bottles (750 ml each) fruity white wine such as
    pinot gris or pinot grigio

25 sprigs thyme

2 teaspoons crushed cardamom pods

1 medium lemon, sliced

1 medium orange, sliced

Combine the sugar and wine in a large saucepan over medium-high heat, stirring occasionally. Once the sugar dissolves, add the thyme, cardamom, lemon and orange slices (reserving a few of each for garnish). Simmer for 30 minutes. Remove from the heat, strain, and discard the solids. Pour into a large pitcher and garnish with reserved citrus slices. Serve in wine glasses.

Ye Olde Grog

Ahoy, maties! Grog has a long, colorful history as sailors' drink of choice. Back in the 1700s, members of the British Royal Navy were allotted a daily ration of rum. When drunkenness became a problem they were ordered to dilute the rum with water, creating the drink known as grog. But don't be fooled—it still packs quite a punch!

FOR EACH DRINK:

1 1/2 **ounces spiced rum**

1 **teaspoon freshly squeezed lemon juice**

1/2 **teaspoon brown sugar**

1 **cup boiling water**

Strip of candied lemon peel for garnish (see page 15)

In a glass mug, mix the rum, lemon juice, and brown sugar until the sugar dissolves. Slowly stir in the boiling water, garnish with candied lemon peel, and serve.

Caramel Apple Sips

We both grew up in Michigan, *where autumn is the most beautiful time of year. Trips to the apple orchard and the caramel dipping sessions that followed are among our fondest memories. Even as grown-ups we love the flavor combination of rich caramel and sweet, juicy apples. We think you will, too.*

4 cups apple cider

1 1/2 cups caramel sauce

4 caramel-dipped Popsicle sticks for garnish (see page 15)

Bring the cider to a simmer in a medium saucepan over medium-high heat. Add the caramel sauce and whisk until melted. Remove from the heat, pour into mugs, garnish with caramel-dipped Popsicle sticks, and serve.

Orange Cardamom Coffee

The sweet-spicy flavor of cardamom combines with zesty

citrus in this rich, fragrant coffee drink.

Seeds from 2 cardamom pods
1/2 cup whole coffee beans
1/2 teaspoon ground cinnamon
1/4 teaspoon ground nutmeg
4 cups cold water
6 ounces (3/4 cup) Grand Marnier (optional)

GARNISH

Whipped cream
Grated orange zest

Grind the cardamom seeds and coffee beans together in a coffee grinder. Using a standard coffeemaker, spoon the coffee/cardamom mixture into a coffee filter. Sprinkle the cinnamon and nutmeg atop the coffee grounds. Pour cold water into the coffeemaker and brew.

Divide the coffee and Grand Marnier, if desired, among 4 mugs and stir. Top each with a dollop of whipped cream, sprinkle with orange zest, and serve.

HOT HINT:

Use whole cardamom seeds rather than ground cardamom, as ground spices quickly lose their essential oils.

Chipotle Chocolate

A dinner party of tapas and other zesty fare provides *the perfect change of pace to the hearty, savory meals of the season. Chipotle powder, which can be found at most Latin American groceries or specialty food markets, gives this spicy hot chocolate a surprising kick that is a fittingly* **fabuloso** *way to end the evening.*

4 cups whole milk

1 1/3 cups semisweet chocolate chips

1/2 to 1 teaspoon chipotle powder, to taste

1/2 teaspoon ground cinnamon

Bring the milk to a simmer in a medium saucepan over medium to medium-high heat. Add the chocolate, chipotle powder, and cinnamon, whisking until the chocolate has melted. Simmer for 1 minute, whisking continuously. Remove from the heat, pour into mugs, and serve.

S'more Meltaways

Hayrides complete with roaring bonfires and campfire treats
are a great way to spend cool autumn nights. Now you don't
necessarily need a campfire to savor the sweetness and gooeyness
of a s'more. Use your broiler or kitchen torch to create this deliciously
sippable version.

GARNISH

Crushed graham crackers
Mini-marshmallows
Melted milk chocolate

4 servings Hot Cocolat (page 41)
1 teaspoon ground cinnamon

To make the garnish: Preheat the broiler. Spread crushed graham crackers on a baking sheet in the shape of 4 circles slightly smaller than the mouths of your mugs (wide-mouthed mugs are preferable). Top with a generous layer of marshmallows and set aside.

Prepare the Hot Cocolat, adding the ground cinnamon during the final minute of simmering, whisking continuously. Pour into the mugs and set aside.

(continued)

Place the baking sheet under the broiler until the marshmallows are toasted and gooey, about 30 seconds. Remove the sheet from the broiler and, using a spatula, lift a marshmallow garnish and place onto a mug of Hot Cocolat, marshmallow side down. Repeat with the remaining garnishes. Drizzle with melted chocolate and serve.

HOT HINT:

A kitchen torch is another quick and easy way to toast the marshmallows for this sweet treat. Just top the Hot Cocolat with marshmallows and heat them with the flame until toasted and gooey. Sprinkle with crushed graham crackers, drizzle with melted chocolate, and serve.

Cranberry Cornucopia

Inspired by a recipe from Gourmet *magazine,* *this mulled tea is one of our favorite sips. The combination of cranberry, anise, and spiced rum provides a cornucopia of flavor. Star anise can be found at most specialty grocers or local Asian markets.*

5 cups water

12 cranberry apple tea bags

1 cup brown sugar

2 1/2 cups cranberry juice

12 whole star anise

Zest of 1 orange, cut into strips

4 cups strained orange juice

3 1/2 cups spiced rum

12 lemon slices for garnish

Bring the water to a boil in a large saucepan. Remove from the heat, add the tea bags, and cover. Steep for 5 minutes.

Remove the tea bags and add the brown sugar, cranberry juice, star anise, and orange zest. Bring the mixture to a boil over medium-high heat. Reduce the heat and simmer for 10 minutes. Add the orange juice and rum and stir until warm. Remove from the heat and strain, reserving the star anise. Ladle into mugs, garnish with star anise and lemon slices, and serve.

Serves 12

Mulled, Mulled Wine

Nip Jack Frost right back
in the nose with a warm, fragrant mug of this spiced wine.

3/4 **cup sugar**

3 **bottles (750 ml each) medium- or full-bodied red wine, such as cabernet or merlot**

5 **cinnamon sticks**

1 **whole nutmeg**

15 **whole cloves**

1 1/2 **teaspoons whole allspice berries**

6 **strips orange zest**

2 **ounces brandy** (optional)

Combine the sugar and wine in a large saucepan over medium-high heat, stirring until the sugar dissolves. Add the spices and orange zest and bring to a simmer. Continue simmering for 1 hour. Remove from the heat, strain, and discard the solids. Add the brandy, if desired. Ladle into mugs or wine glasses and serve.

Witches' Brew

Want to have the coolest Halloween spookfest on the block?
*Transform your typical party punch into a haunted witches' brew by
spicing it up and serving it atop dry ice with some floating
eyeballs (a.k.a. peeled grapes). With a party this cool, who needs trick-or-treating!*

8 cups grape juice
16 whole cloves
4 cinnamon sticks
1/8 teaspoon ground nutmeg
Peeled grapes, for garnish
Dry ice

Combine the grape juice, cloves, cinnamon sticks, and nutmeg
in a large saucepan over medium-high heat and bring to a simmer. Reduce the heat to medium-low and simmer for 5 minutes.

Meanwhile, break apart a piece of dry ice with an ice pick (do
not use your hands). Place a few chunks in a large cauldron and
cover with water. Place a metal bowl inside the cauldron and
strain in the warm juice mixture and peeled grapes. Ladle into
mugs and serve immediately, as the dry ice can cool down
the brew.

HOT HINT:

**Be sure to have an adult do the ladling, as the dry ice can burn
bare hands.**

CLASSIC HOLIDAY DRINKS

It's the most wonderful time of the year. And this collection of recipes will make it the hot-hottiest season of all. These classic holiday drinks are sure to turn your Merry Christmas into a Merry Mix-mas.

Hang the lights, trim the tree, and sing with Bing as you share a bowl of Sugarplum Punch or sip a warm Gingerbread Man. After a long day of shopping for everything on Santa's list, invite friends over to decompress with Praline Prancers and Coquitos. Or start a tradition by hosting an annual gift-wrapping or cookie-baking session, complete with a batch of spiked Eggnog. Whether you've been naughty or nice, these holiday hotties are sure to make you the hostess with the mostest! You'll transform your guests' inner Grinch, as you entertain with these amazing seasonal sippers. So have yourself a merry little mix-mas time!

Eggnog

A descendant of Old World milk and wine punches, *eggnog became a popular social drink in nineteenth-century England, where it was served in large quantities at holiday parties, usually to toast one's health. Americans were the first to add rum, also known as grog, hence the name eggnog. While people may be accustomed to drinking their eggnog chilled, we find it's even yummier when warm.*

12 cups whole milk

12 eggs

1 1/2 cups sugar

3/4 teaspoon ground cinnamon

3/4 teaspoon ground nutmeg

1 tablespoon vanilla extract

3 cups dark rum (optional)

Freshly grated nutmeg for garnish

Bring the milk to a simmer in a large saucepan over medium-high heat. Meanwhile, in a medium bowl, combine the eggs, sugar, cinnamon, nutmeg, and vanilla. Add 1 cup of the simmering milk to the egg mixture, stirring to combine.

Whisk the milk-and-egg mixture into the simmering milk in the saucepan. Simmer for 1 minute, whisking continuously. Remove from the heat and add the rum, if desired. Ladle into mugs, garnish each with a dusting of nutmeg, and serve.

HOT HINT:

Not feeling rummy? Use bourbon in place of the rum for a Southern flair, or omit the alcohol and add 2 2/3 cups unsweetened cocoa powder for a chocolaty version perfect for the little ones.

Praline Prancers

You know Dasher and Dancer and Prancer and Vixen,

but do you recall the most famous holiday
cocktail of all? No, it's not a Rudolph,

it's a Praline Prancer! The warm, nutty flavor of the
"prah-leen" may even give you a red nose!

BROWN SUGAR RIM

Equal parts Frangelico and amaretto, combined
Brown sugar

6 ounces (3/4 cup) Frangelico
6 ounces (3/4 cup) amaretto
2 tablespoons brown sugar
2 tablespoons unsalted butter

Dip the edges of 4 martini glasses in the liqueurs and rim them
with brown sugar.

Combine the 12 ounces of Frangelico and amaretto liqueurs,
2 tablespoons brown sugar, and the butter in a small saucepan
over medium heat. Stir until the butter has melted and the
sugar has dissolved. Continue heating until the mixture is warm
but not hot. Remove from the heat, pour into the rimmed
martini glasses, and serve.

Wassail Bowl

Ves heill! Norsemen feasting and drinking at yuletide celebrations raised their glasses with this old toast, which means "be in good health." Serve this spiced holiday brew from a traditional wassail bowl and garnish with small roasted apples to create your own midwinter festival.

GARNISH

6 small to medium apples

5 teaspoons brown sugar

1 teaspoon ground cinnamon

9 cups amber ale

2 cups sweet sherry

1 1/2 cups brown sugar

6 whole cloves

6 whole allspice berries

1 cinnamon stick

1 1/2 teaspoons ground ginger

3/4 teaspoon ground nutmeg

To make the garnish: Preheat the oven to 350°F. Core the apples and place them in a small baking pan. Combine the brown sugar and cinnamon in a small bowl and fill each apple with 1 teaspoon of the mixture. Add water to cover the bottom of the pan and bake until the apples are soft, about 30 minutes. Remove from the oven. When the apples are cool enough to handle, cut 2 of them into thin slices and set aside.

Combine the ale, sherry, brown sugar, and spices in a large saucepan and simmer over medium heat for 15 minutes. Remove from the heat, strain, and discard the solids. Serve in a wassail bowl or any large punch bowl, floating the 4 apples on top. Ladle into mugs and garnish each with apple slices.

Serves 4

Gingerbread Men

Nothing signals the holidays more than frosted gingerbread houses or *yummy gingerbread cookies. Capture the spirit with the sweet, spicy flavor of this coffee-based concoction. And you can keep these little guys around for a while, since the gingerbread syrup lasts in the fridge for up to a week.*

GINGERBREAD SYRUP

1/3 cup molasses

2 1/2 tablespoons brown sugar

3/4 teaspoon baking soda

1 teaspoon ground ginger

1/4 teaspoon ground cinnamon

1/4 teaspoon ground cloves, plus extra for garnish

4 cups freshly brewed strong coffee

4 tablespoons half-and-half

Whipped cream for garnish

To make the gingerbread syrup: In a small bowl, mix the molasses, brown sugar, baking soda, and spices. Cover and refrigerate for at least 10 minutes.

Pour 1/2 cup coffee and 1 tablespoon gingerbread syrup into each of 4 mugs, stirring until the syrup dissolves. Add 1 tablespoon half-and-half and an additional 1/2 cup coffee to each mug. Serve with a dollop of whipped cream and a dusting of ground cloves.

Ponche

This classic Mexican holiday ponche *takes a bit more effort than most, but it's worth it, as the unique flavor blend is a nice alternative to standard holiday punches. The fruits, which may be fresh or frozen, can be found at most Latin American groceries. And with a touch of tequila, you and your guests will be living* la vida loca.

2 apples, peeled, cored, and thickly sliced, plus star
  shapes cut from apple slices for garnish (see page 16)

3/4 cup raisins

1 pound of guavas, quartered

Twelve 1-inch cubes sugar cane, cut into strips

1/2 cup prunes

8 ounces crabapples, peeled

1/2 cup brown sugar

1/2 cup granulated sugar

4 cinnamon sticks

1 gallon water

2 1/4 cups tequila (optional)

Combine all the ingredients except the tequila and apple garnish in a stockpot. Bring to a boil over medium-high heat. Reduce the heat and simmer for 2 hours. Remove from the heat, strain into a punch bowl, and discard the solids. Add the tequila, if desired. Ladle into punch cups, garnish with apple stars, and serve.

Coquitos

In Puerto Rico, they add coconut milk to their holiday eggnog.
Served with colorful drink umbrellas or bamboo-skewered
pineapple slices, Coquitos provide a truly tropical feel,
which will be welcomed come the middle of winter.

3 cups 2 percent or whole milk

1 cup coconut milk

1/2 cup brown sugar

1/8 teaspoon ground cinnamon

1/8 teaspoon freshly grated nutmeg

1 teaspoon vanilla extract

4 ounces (1/2 cup) dark rum

Heat the milk in a medium saucepan over medium to medium-high heat. Stir in the coconut milk, brown sugar, spices, and vanilla, and continue heating until steaming but not simmering. Remove from the heat and pour into Irish coffee glasses. Add 1 ounce of rum to each glass, stir, and serve.

Sugarplum Punch

Visions of sugarplums may be dancing in your head, but after
a few sips of Sugarplum Punch your tastebuds will be dancing, too.

SUGAR RIM

White grape juice
Sugar

6 cups prune juice
6 cups white grape juice
3 cups peach nectar
6 cinnamon sticks
1 teaspoon whole cloves
1 teaspoon crushed cardamom pods

Dip the rims of 12 glass punch cups in white grape juice, and rim
them with sugar.

Combine all the ingredients in a large saucepan and bring to a
boil over medium-high heat. Reduce the heat to medium-low
and simmer for 10 minutes. Remove from the heat, strain, and
discard the solids. Ladle into the sugar-rimmed punch cups
and serve.

Serves 12

• • •

Glögg

Traditionally served during Advent, *this Scandinavian spiced wine is a wonderful way to warm up on a cold winter's eve. Its smooth, rich flavor is perfectly complemented by the nuttiness of the almonds.*

1 bottle (750 ml) ruby port

1 bottle (750 ml) sweet white wine, such as muscat or Sauternes

1 bottle (750 ml) sweet sherry

1 1/2 cups dry, full-bodied red wine, such as chianti or Burgundy

16 whole cloves

1 1/2 teaspoons crushed cardamom pods

1 cinnamon stick

1 cup sugar

4 ounces (1/2 cup) brandy

GARNISH

1/2 cup raisins

1/2 cup dried figs, quartered

1 cup slivered almonds

Combine all the ingredients (except the garnish) in a large saucepan and simmer over medium heat for 15 minutes. Remove from the heat, strain, and discard the solids.

Ladle into mugs, garnish with the raisins, figs, and almonds, and serve.

Serves 12

Hallie's Glühwein

The Christmas-keeping Germans are famous for their Weihnachtsmarkt
—*winter markets*
*where ornaments, wreaths, and other Christmas items are sold. Shoppers keep warm
and happy with Glühwein, a spiced wine drink. This tea-based
version is a favorite of Katie's Grandma Hallie, who serves
it at Christmastime.*

4 1/2 cups water

2/3 cup honey

1/2 cup brown sugar

1/4 cup minced peeled fresh ginger

1 1/2 teaspoons whole cloves

1 teaspoon whole allspice berries

2 vanilla beans, chopped

2 Earl Grey tea bags

2 bottles (750 ml each) dry, full-bodied red wine
   such as chianti or Burgundy

4 ounces (1/2 cup) whiskey

Combine the water, honey, brown sugar, ginger, cloves, allspice,
and vanilla beans in a large saucepan. Bring the mixture to a
boil over medium-high heat, stirring until the honey and sugar
dissolve. Reduce the heat and simmer for 5 minutes. Remove
from the heat. Add the tea bags, cover, and steep for 5 minutes.
Remove the tea bags, add the wine, and heat until warm. Remove
from the heat, strain, and discard the solids. Ladle into mugs,
add a splash of whiskey to each mug, and serve.

White Hot Mint

Rich white chocolate is so yummy
with a hint of mint. Dressed up in green for the holidays
and swizzled with a candy cane, this drink has quite the festive flair.

4 cups whole milk

3/4 cup chopped white chocolate

4 ounces (1/2 cup) crème de menthe liqueur or crème de menthe syrup (such as Torani)

Miniature candy canes for garnish

Bring the milk to a simmer in a medium saucepan over medium to medium-high heat. Add the white chocolate, whisking until melted. Remove from the heat, stir in the crème de menthe, and pour into Irish coffee glasses. Serve with candy canes.

HOT HINT:

For a Peppermint Patty, replace the white chocolate with milk chocolate or semisweet chocolate.

Tom & Jerry

After hitting the slopes, there's nothing like sitting in front of a roaring fire and sipping a rich, steaming Tom & Jerry. But you don't have to visit an Aspen ski lodge to enjoy this classic. Whip up a batch in the comfort of your own home and invite over some friends.

14 ounces (1 3/4 cups) brandy

12 ounces (1 1/2 cups) spiced rum

6 eggs, separated

3/4 cup superfine sugar

Pinch of ground cinnamon

Pinch of ground allspice

Pinch of ground cloves

12 cups whole milk

Freshly grated nutmeg for garnish

Into each of 12 mugs, pour 1 ounce of brandy and 1 ounce of spiced rum. Set aside.

In a mixer, beat the egg yolks and sugar until lemon colored and runny. Do not overbeat (if fluffy, they're overbeaten). Slowly stir in the cinnamon, allspice, cloves, and remaining 2 ounces of brandy. Mix well and set aside.

Heat the milk in a medium saucepan over medium heat until warm but not simmering.

Meanwhile, beat the egg whites in a mixer until they form a stiff froth. Fold the whites into the yolk mixture (if the yolk mixture has separated, whisk to blend).

Add 2 tablespoons of the egg mixture to each mug and stir. Pour 1 cup of warm milk into each mug and stir until frothy. Sprinkle each mug with nutmeg and serve.

NOTE:

Raw eggs should not be used in food prepared for pregnant women, babies, young children, the elderly, or anyone whose health is compromised.

New Year's Toast

Parties with a signature cocktail are a great way to entertain.
*So for your next New Year's fete, serve up this effervescent
potion. It's an interesting twist on the traditional bubbly!*

3 cups white grape juice
1 bottle (750 ml) champagne, at room temperature
2 ounces pomegranate juice, at room temperature
Raspberries for garnish

Heat the white grape juice in a small saucepan over medium-high
heat until steaming but not simmering. Into each of 8 champagne flutes, pour 3 ounces champagne, 3 ounces white grape
juice, and a generous splash of pomegranate juice. Drop in a
raspberry or two and serve.

Serves 1

Mistletoe Mist

If you have too much of this minty drink, *who knows*
whom you'll kiss under the mistletoe!

FOR EACH DRINK:

1 teaspoon sugar

8 fresh mint leaves

Splash of tonic water

1/2 cup cranberry juice

1 ounce gin

**Sugared cranberries on a skewer
for garnish** (see page 17)

Gently crush the sugar, mint, and tonic water in an Irish coffee glass, using a muddler or the back of a wooden spoon. Combine the cranberry juice and gin in a small saucepan and heat over medium heat until steaming but not simmering. Add the cranberry juice mixture to the mint mixture and stir. Strain into a fresh Irish coffee glass, discard the mint, and serve garnished with a sugared cranberry skewer.

FESTIVE
AFTER-DINNER
DRINKS

Nothing adds a bit of elegance to a dinner party or tops off a night at The Nutcracker *better than an assortment of after-dinner drinks. These post-supper sippers will provide the perfect final touch to any evening.*

Looking for a fitting finale to your next family holiday celebration? Instead of slaving over a *bûche de Noël*, make a sinfully rich dessert drink. Who can resist the delicious flavors of Tiramisù or Dulce de Leche? Or rather than capping off your night with the same old decaf, impress your guests with a Hazelnut Truffle. Whichever liquid finale you choose, it's destined to be a sweet ending.

Tiramisù

The English translation of the Italian tiramisù *is "pick me up."*
Indulge in its light, creamy
texture and unforgettable flavor trio of chocolate, coffee, and rum, and you will
actually feel as if you have been picked up . . . and dropped off in heaven!

KAHLÚA WHIPPED CREAM

1 cup heavy whipping cream
2 tablespoons sugar
¹/₂ ounce Kahlúa

4 cups 2 percent or whole milk
2 cups shaved bittersweet chocolate
¹/₄ cup espresso powder or instant coffee
3 ounces (¹/₃ cup) dark rum
Ladyfinger cookies for serving

To make the Kahlúa whipped cream: In a medium bowl, beat the whipping cream, sugar, and Kahlúa until peaks form. It can be prepared 1 day ahead and stored in the refrigerator; whisk before serving. Makes 2 cups.

Bring the milk to a simmer in a medium saucepan over medium heat. Add the chocolate and whisk until melted. Simmer for 1 minute, whisking continuously. Remove from the heat and pour into 4 mugs. Add 1 tablespoon espresso powder and 1 tablespoon plus 1 teaspoon rum to each mug, stirring well. Top with a dollop of Kahlúa whipped cream and serve with ladyfinger cookies. Reserve the remaining whipped cream for another use.

Serves 1

Café Dolores

Holly's grandma, Dolores, was a wonderful cook who spent
hours in the kitchen making meals for her family and friends to enjoy.
One of her greatest pleasures was a good cup of coffee.
This blend of coffee, rum, and chocolate is named in her honor.

TÍA MARIA WHIPPED CREAM

1 cup heavy whipping cream
2 tablespoons sugar
1/2 ounce Tía Maria

FOR EACH DRINK:

3/4 cup freshly brewed coffee
1/2 ounce dark rum
1/2 ounce Tía Maria
1/2 ounce dark crème de cacao

To make the Tía Maria whipped cream: In a medium bowl, beat the whipping cream, sugar, and Tía Maria until peaks form. It can be prepared 1 day ahead and stored in the refrigerator; whisk before serving. Makes 2 cups.

Combine the coffee, rum, Tía Maria, and crème de cacao in an Irish coffee glass and stir. Top with a dollop of Tía Maria whipped cream and serve. Reserve the remaining whipped cream for another use.

Kiss Me I'm Irish Coffee

Joe Sheridan concocted this classic to warm and awaken airplane passengers
arriving at Ireland's Sheridan Airport. San Francisco newspaper
columnist Stanton Delaplane loved it so much that he brought it home
to his neighborhood bar, the Buena Vista Tavern. Now you can bring it home, too.

FOR EACH DRINK:

2 teaspoons sugar

1 1/2 ounces Irish whiskey

2/3 cup freshly brewed strong black coffee

1 tablespoon heavy whipping cream

Combine the sugar, whiskey, and coffee in an Irish coffee glass.
In a small bowl, lightly whisk the cream until slightly frothy.
Gently pour the cream onto the back of a spoon resting on the
surface of the coffee, so that it floats on top of the coffee.
Serve without stirring.

HOT HINT:

Getting the cream to float on top of an Irish coffee may require a little
luck of the Irish. To ensure success, don't omit the sugar, even if you
typically don't take it in your coffee, and remember not to stir in the
cream, as the secret to experiencing the true flavor of an Irish coffee
is sipping it through the floating cream.

Hazelnut Truffles

Chocolate and hazelnut—*a match made in heaven.*
These flavors combine for an elegant ending to your holiday dinner party!

CHOCOLATE RIM

Equal parts Frangelico and Godiva liqueur, combined
Shaved milk chocolate or semisweet chocolate

6 ounces (3/4 cup) Frangelico
6 ounces (3/4 cup) Godiva liqueur

Dip the edges of 4 martini glasses in the liqueurs and rim them with chocolate.

In a small saucepan, combine the 12 ounces of Frangelico and Godiva liqueur. Heat over medium to medium-high heat until warm but not hot. Pour into the rimmed martini glasses and serve.

HOT HINT:

This is one of those recipes where a spouted or lipped-rim saucepan comes in handy. If you don't have such a pan, transfer the hot liquid to a glass measuring cup. This will make it much easier to pour the mixture into the rimmed glasses without spilling or disturbing the pretty chocolate rim.

Chocolate Raspberry Kiss

Spend Valentine's Day with your honey and this heart-stopping hot drink. Who knew you could capture love in a mug?

1 1/2 cups freshly brewed coffee

3 tablespoons semisweet chocolate chips

4 ounces (1/2 cup) Chambord

2 ounces (1/4 cup) Godiva liqueur

GARNISH

Whipped cream

Unsweetened cocoa powder

Red-tinted sugar (see page 17)

Combine the coffee and chocolate in a small saucepan over medium-low heat and whisk until the chocolate has melted. Remove from the heat and pour into 2 mugs. Add 2 ounces Chambord and 1 ounce Godiva liqueur to each mug, stirring to combine.

Top with a dollop of whipped cream, sprinkle with cocoa powder and red sugar, and serve.

HOT HINT:

Instead of serving plain old coffee at your next gathering, set up a coffee bar where guests can create their own custom concoctions. Brew up regular and decaf coffee, about two 6-ounce cups per guest, and serve in an urn or percolator. Along with the standard cream and sugar, set out a variety of liqueurs, such as Baileys and Kahlúa, as well as whipped cream with cocoa and spices for dusting.

Serves 4

...

Bananas Foster

The quintessential New Orleans dessert,
Bananas Foster was created in 1951 in the heart of the French Quarter. Whip up some voodoo and serve this liquid version for a fabulous ending to your next bayou and blues bash.

4 cups 2 percent or whole milk
1/2 cup plus 2 tablespoons caramel sauce
4 ounces (1/2 cup) crème de banane
2 teaspoons vanilla extract

GARNISH

Whipped cream
Caramel sauce for drizzling

Combine the milk and caramel sauce in a medium saucepan over medium-high heat and whisk until the caramel has melted. Continue heating until steaming but not simmering. Remove from the heat and pour into 4 mugs. Add 1 ounce crème de banane and 1/2 teaspoon vanilla to each mug.

Top with a dollop of whipped cream, drizzle with caramel sauce, and serve.

Serves 4

Root Beer Floats

A frosty root beer float
*is one of summer's best pleasures. But why wait until then
to enjoy that sweet, creamy flavor you love? Served with
a foamy rim, this is a fun and yummy warm treat.*

6 ounces (3/4 cup) Kahlúa
6 ounces (3/4 cup) anisette
3/4 cup half-and-half
Whipped cream for garnish

Combine the Kahlúa, anisette, and half-and-half in a small saucepan and heat over medium to medium-high heat until warm but not hot.

Dip the rims of 4 small glass mugs into a shallow dish of whipped cream to create a foamy rim. Pour the mixture into the rimmed mugs, being careful to avoid the whipped cream, and serve.

Café Monk

B & B is a blend of cognac and Benedictine, *a liqueur named after the sixteenth-century French Benedictine monks who created it. Its delicate herbal fragrance and flavor are lovely in this coffee concoction.*

FOR EACH DRINK:

3/4 **cup freshly brewed coffee**
3/4 **ounce Kahlúa**
3/4 **ounce B & B**
Splash of Grand Marnier

GARNISH

Whipped cream
Grated orange zest

Combine the coffee, Kahlúa, B & B, and Grand Marnier in an Irish coffee glass and stir. Top with a dollop of whipped cream, sprinkle with orange zest, and serve.

Serves 2 or 4

. . .

Dulce de Leche

Go south of the border for this rich caramel drink. *Based on the favorite Latin American confection, this recipe makes two truly rich servings or can be split among demitasse cups for small sweet treats.*

1 cup 2 percent or whole milk
2/3 cup sweetened condensed milk
1/2 ounce dark rum (optional)

Heat the milk in a small saucepan over medium-high heat. Whisk in the condensed milk until completely blended. Continue heating until the mixture is steaming but not simmering. Remove from the heat, add the rum, if desired, pour into 2 mugs or 4 demitasse cups, and serve.

COZY CUPS

The presents have been opened and the last guests have finally said goodnight! Wind down from the holiday craziness or just relax after a stressful day with the warmth of a cozy cup.

Keep yourself going at the holiday party with a Mocha Almond Latte. And what better way to end your busy day than with a warm, sweet Nightcapper or a scrumptious Snowslide. Whether it's morning, noon, or night, wrap your fingers around a mug, cozy up by the fire, and sip something simmering.

Mocha Almond Latte

Don't run out to the local coffee house to satisfy your java craving. Making lattes and other flavored coffee drinks at home is quick and easy. Just brew up some coffee, select your flavors, and blend. A topping of whipped cream makes it sublime!

FOR EACH DRINK:

1/2 **cup freshly brewed coffee**

1/2 **cup 2 percent or whole milk, warmed**

3/4 **ounce amaretto**

3/4 **ounce dark crème de cacao**

GARNISH

Whipped cream

Shaved chocolate

Sliced almonds

Combine the coffee, milk, amaretto, and crème de cacao in a latte cup and stir. Top with a dollop of whipped cream, sprinkle with chocolate and almonds, and serve.

Spiced Chai Tea

Recipes for chai are as individual as our lists for Santa.
We've used our favorite spices to create this zesty, full-flavored
version, but feel free to experiment and create your very own blend,
with spices such as cardamom, allspice, and star anise.

2 cups water

1/4 teaspoon whole black peppercorns

6 whole cloves

1 cinnamon stick

3 to 4 pinches freshly grated nutmeg

1 teaspoon minced peeled fresh ginger

1/2 vanilla bean, finely chopped

2 teaspoons Darjeeling or similar black tea leaves

2 cups 2 percent or whole milk

1/2 cup honey

Bring the water to a boil in a medium saucepan. Stir in the spices, vanilla bean, and tea leaves. Cover, remove from the heat, and steep for 15 minutes. Add the milk and warm the mixture over medium heat until steaming but not simmering. Remove from the heat, strain, and pour into 4 mugs, discarding the solids. Stir 2 tablespoons of honey into each mug and serve.

HOT HINT:

Combine the spices, vanilla bean, and tea leaves ahead of time and store in an airtight container. With the blend at your fingertips, you can easily prepare chai any time.

Serves 4
. . .

Nightcappers

When it's time for a long winter's nap,
cuddle up with this celestial blend of green tea and Chambord.
And once the weather warms up, try putting it on ice.
The refreshing flavor is reminiscent of raspberry iced tea.

3 cups freshly brewed green tea

4 teaspoons honey

8 ounces (1 cup) Chambord

Combine 3/4 cup tea, 1 teaspoon honey, and 2 ounces Chambord in each of 4 mugs. Stir until the honey is dissolved and serve.

Lavender Vanilla Cream

Nothing is more comforting *during the hectic holidays than*
cuddling up in your favorite chair and sipping a warm drink.
This fragrant milk, with just a hint of lavender, is a soothing
drink before bedtime or the perfect complement to a morning biscuit.

FOR EACH DRINK:

1 1/3 cups 2 percent or whole milk
4 teaspoons Lavender Sugar (recipe follows)
1/4 teaspoon vanilla extract

Heat the milk and lavender sugar in a small saucepan over
medium-low heat for 15 minutes, being careful not to boil.
Remove from the heat, strain into a mug, and discard the
solids. Stir in the vanilla and serve.

LAVENDER SUGAR:

Combine 1 cup sugar and 2 tablespoons dried lavender flowers
in a small bowl. Store in an airtight container for at least 2 days
and up to a few months.

HOT HINT:

Leftover lavender sugar can be used in lemonade or in baked goods,
or you can sprinkle it on cakes, cookies, and fresh fruit.

Serves 4

Berry White

The flavors of raspberries and white chocolate blend together *beautifully in this smoother-than-smooth concoction. Just one sip and you'll be saying you're the first, you're the last,*

my everydrink.

3 cups 2 percent or whole milk

1 cup chopped white chocolate

6 ounces (3/4 cup) Chambord

2 tablespoons raspberry syrup (such as Torani)

Mixed berries, such as blueberries or raspberries, on a skewer for garnish

Bring the milk to a simmer in a medium saucepan over medium to medium-high heat. Add the chocolate and whisk until melted. Continue heating until steaming but not simmering, whisking continuously. Remove from the heat and stir in the Chambord and raspberry syrup. Pour into mugs and serve garnished with skewered berries.

Snowslides

A Mudslide over ice is a hit in the summer, *but its warmer relative,*
the Snowslide, is also irresistibly delicious.
You'll want to keep this creamy cocktail flowing all winter long.

4 ounces (1/2 cup) Kahlúa
4 ounces (1/2 cup) Baileys Irish Cream
4 ounces (1/2 cup) vodka
1 1/3 cups 2 percent or whole milk

SNOWFLAKE STENCIL

Whipped cream
Unsweetened cocoa powder

Combine the Kahlúa, Baileys, vodka, and milk in a small saucepan
over medium or medium-high heat until steaming but not simmering. Remove from the heat and pour into 4 Irish coffee glasses.
Garnish with cocoa snowflake stencils using the whipped cream
and cocoa powder (see page 16), and serve.

Heavenly Hibiscus

In the mood for a taste of the tropics?
Mellow out with a warm mug of Heavenly Hibiscus. Pineapple,
coconut, and ginger combine with hibiscus flowers to form a lovely
violet concoction that tastes as wonderful as it looks!

FOR EACH DRINK:

1/2 **cup water**

1/2 **cup pineapple juice**

1/2 **cup coconut milk**

1 **tablespoon dried hibiscus flowers**

1/8 **teaspoon ground ginger**

Ginger slice cut into flower shapes, skewered,
for garnish (see page 16)

Combine the water, pineapple juice, coconut milk, hibiscus
flowers, and ground ginger in a small saucepan over medium-
high heat and bring to a boil. Reduce the heat and simmer
for 5 minutes. Strain into a mug and discard the solids. Serve
with skewered ginger flowers.

Malted Milk Mug

If you love the rich flavor of malt as much as we do,
you'll love this cocoa. Drop in a malted milk ball for a touch of whimsy.

FOR EACH DRINK:

1 tablespoon unsweetened cocoa powder
1 1/2 tablespoons sugar
3 tablespoons malt powder
1 cup 2 percent or whole milk
Malted milk ball for garnish

Mix the cocoa powder, sugar, and malt powder together in a small bowl. Bring the milk to a simmer in a small saucepan over medium heat. Slowly stir in the cocoa mixture until completely dissolved. Simmer for 1 minute, stirring continuously. Remove from the heat and pour into a mug. Drop in a malted milk ball and serve.

Lemon Ginger Tea

The tartness of the lemon complements the ginger in this
wonderfully pungent brew. Garnished with
a sparkling candied lemon peel, this tea is as pretty as it is invigorating.

FOR EACH DRINK:

1 cup water

1-inch piece fresh ginger, peeled and minced

1 tablespoon freshly squeezed lemon juice

1/2 teaspoon honey

1/2 ounce Lemon-Flavored Vodka
(recipe follows; optional)

1/2 ounce anisette (optional)

**Strip of candied lemon peel for
garnish** (see page 15)

Combine the water, ginger, and lemon juice in a small saucepan over medium-high heat and bring to a boil. Cover, remove from the heat, and steep for 5 minutes. Strain into a mug and discard the solids. Add the honey and stir until dissolved. Add the vodka and anisette, if desired. Serve in a mug or teacup with a strip of candied lemon peel.

LEMON-FLAVORED VODKA:

Place the zest of 1 lemon (removed in strips) inside a 1-pint (375 ml) bottle of vodka. You may need to pour out a small amount of the vodka to make room for the lemon zest. Seal tightly and let stand at room temperature for 1 week. Shake the bottle every few days. Strain and discard the solids and use.

Index

Liquid Measurements

- **Bar spoon** = $1/2$ ounce
- **1 teaspoon** = $1/6$ ounce
- **1 tablespoon** = $1/2$ ounce
- **2 tablespoons** (pony) = 1 ounce
- **3 tablespoons** (jigger) = $1\,1/2$ ounces
- **$1/4$ cup** = 2 ounces
- **$1/3$ cup** = 3 ounces
- **$1/2$ cup** = 4 ounces
- **$2/3$ cup** = 5 ounces
- **$3/4$ cup** = 6 ounces
- **1 cup** = 8 ounces
- **1 pint** = 16 ounces
- **1 quart** = 32 ounces
- **750 ml bottle** = 25.4 ounces
- **1 liter bottle** = 33.8 ounces

- **1 medium lemon** = 3 tablespoons juice
- **1 medium lime** = 2 tablespoons juice
- **1 medum orange** = $1/3$ cup juice